CHANGING YOUR LIFE THROUGH A POSITIVE ATTITUDE

I0157975

The 30-Day Challenge

by Lorena Laughlin

CLADD
PUBLISHING

Cladd Publishing Inc.
USA

This publication is designed to provide accurate information
regarding the subject matter covered. It is sold with the
understanding that neither the author nor the publisher is
providing medical, legal or other professional advice or
services. Always seek advice from a competent professional
before using any of the information in this book. The author
and the publisher specifically disclaim any liability that is
incurred from the use or application of the contents of this
book.

Changing Your Life Through a Positive Attitude: The 30 Day
Challenge

ISBN 978-1-946881-06-9 (e-book)
ISBN 978-1-946881-15-1 (paperback)

Contents

Chapter 1: The Root of Your Unhappiness

When it comes to success and happiness in any endeavor or life in general, it all comes down to the attitude you project out into the world. If your attitude is negative, you will make bad choices, and create unnecessary conflict and problems for yourself. However, when your attitude is coming from an empowering state-of-mind, then this will lead to better decisions that can help you solve problems and take advantage of the opportunities that life presents you with.

Your attitude forms the foundation of everything you desire to be, do, have, and achieve in life. With a positive attitude, the world is your oyster. Without it, your world will be filled with ill fate and unfortunate circumstances.

SELF-PITY

Feeling sorry for yourself will destroy any chances of happiness. Self-pity paralyzes you and leaves you unable to take any action towards improving your situation. There is a distinct difference between acknowledging that you're not where you would like to be, and feeling sorry for yourself. If you are not happy with where you are today, then let go of the self-pity so that you can move forward with no restraints.

NEGLECT

Neglecting to take care of your negative outlook on life can lead to a perilous outcome that can be extremely difficult to climb out from underneath. Neglecting your physical and mental health increases the difficulty of regaining it exponentially with time. Neglecting your positive relationships may mean losing them altogether. Pay attention to the things that are important in your life because failing to do so can have disastrous results.

INDIFFERENCE

You're neither hot nor cold. You simply don't care at all. You're drifting through life directionless that leads you to an undetermined destination. You can't drift your way into success and happiness. To be successful in anything, you must be keenly focus and maintain a positive outlook. Pick a direction and go for it with everything you have. If you're inspired you will have the energy to move mountains.

DOUBT

Doubt is one of the most detrimental negative-attitude syndromes of them all. There are several types of doubt, but self-doubt is the most insidious and damaging. You doubt if you're good enough, smart enough, or talented. You doubt if you're able to reach your goals, and even when you reach an optimal position you doubt if it will continue. Success comes from a positive state-of-mind and self-confidence. The understanding of self-worth will open your world to happiness that you never thought possible.

WORRY

Worrying doesn't solve anything and it contributes to increasing levels of anxiety. Worrying repeatedly and often can reduce you to being presumably doomed for the rest of your life. Completely eradicate it from your everyday thoughts, and you will soon find the benefits are life changing.

PESSIMISM

You go out of your way to find the negative aspects in every situation. The pessimistic mind leads an ugly, terrible life. Spending your precious energy looking for potential reasons why things won't work is a sure way to be miserable and alone.

Perception is reality. Change the way you view things and it will change the direction of your life and increase your happiness instantly. Poor thinking habits lead to living a poor existence.

CLOSE MINDEDNESS

A major problem in today society is the lack of curiosity. Instead of having a know-it-all approach to life, become more curious. Open your mind to new ways of thinking, new types of people, and new experiences. It's impossible to change your life, if you continue to hold onto a closed-mind.

COMPLAINING

When you are whining, crying, moaning, groaning, you have a zero percent chance of having an excellent life. Complaining kills dreams with an unusual efficiency. You complain about the weather, your job, your partner, your kids, your parents; you complain about everything. Stop it! Don't cry about your life, do something about it.

Chapter 2: The Power of Appreciation

Appreciation means thankfulness, counting your blessings, noticing simple pleasures, and acknowledging everything that you receive. It means learning to live your life as if it was a miracle, and being aware on a continuous basis of how much you've been given.

Appreciation shifts your focus from what your life lacks, to the abundance that is already present. In addition, behavioral and psychological research has shown the surprising life improvements that comes from the practice of appreciation. Giving thanks makes people happier and more resilient, it strengthens relationships, it improves health, and it dramatically reduces stress.

Research Shows That Appreciation Heightens Your Quality of Life

Psychologists, of Southern Methodist University in Texas, and the University of California, conducted research on appreciation and its impact on people's well-being. The study split several hundred people into three different groups. All participants were asked to keep daily diaries.

➤ The 1st group kept a diary of the events that occurred during the day without being told specifically to write about.

➤ 2nd group was told to record their unpleasant experiences only.

> ➤ 3rd group was instructed to make a daily list of things for which they were grateful for.

The results of the study have shown that daily appreciation exercises resulted in higher reported levels of alertness, enthusiasm, determination, optimism, and energy.

Those in the appreciation group experienced less depression and stress, were more likely to help others, exercised more regularly, and made greater progress toward achieving personal goals.

Increasing Your Natural Happiness Levels

Practicing appreciation can increase happiness levels up to 25%. This is very important, because your body strives to maintain a basic level of happiness at a predetermined point. If something bad happens to you, your happiness will decrease momentarily, but then it returns to its natural level. Thus, the same happens in reverse if something positive happens, your level of happiness rises, and then it returns once again. Regularly practicing appreciation raises your "natural happiness level" so you can remain at an increased level regardless of outside circumstances.

Research shows that those who strive to maintain heightened happiness levels, tend to be more creative, bounce back more quickly from adversity, have a stronger immune system, and have stronger social relationships than those who don't.

APPRECIATION IS POSITIVE

❖ Appreciation forces you to see only the positive things in your life.

Chapter 3: Being A Victim of Negativity

It is very common to allow yourself to be influenced by other people in your life. In fact, you can also become a victim of negativity through TV, news, social media, and music. Negativity runs ramped through our society and causes a lifetime of damage.

To change and adopt a positive attitude, it will be essential that you kick negativity all together. Negative thoughts are things that we see or hear that makes us feel unhappy, stressed, sad, depressed, scared, ashamed, guilty, angry and so on. If you do not feel good when thinking about them, then they are considered a negative thought.

THE FORMULA FOR ENJOYING A LIFE FULL OF HAPPINESS:

- ❖ A Positive Mind = An Increase in Positive Experiences

Chapter 4: News Creates Fear

Media is in your face every day in almost every single way. It is one of the most challenging habits to kick. We look to the media for our information, friendships, communication, social updates, entertainment and much more. It can consume and destroy your positive outlook on life in seconds.

The local and national news are filled with headlines that are created to grab your attention by any means possible. They create fear and outrage for the sake of their business. This type of negativity has a way of lingering with you for the rest of the day. It is very difficult to stay super positive while you are still thinking about the disturbing news you just watched. After a while you could even begin to believe that the entire world is a sad, disturbing place filled with hatred and violence, even though this is not the truth.

Quick Tip:
Try taking a long break from the media and focus only on yourself and your own attitude towards life.

Chapter 5: Social Media Drives Depression

It is a new norm that arguments or personal issues are aired out on social media for everyone to see. Then to make matters worse, the peanut gallery chimes in and gives their own thoughts on the matter. These types of sites drive depression, fear, and feelings of being completely out of control. You are helpless as long as you are a part of the viscous game.

Quick Tip:
Disconnect and redirect your energy on things that matter. Take the time to join a class, learn a new skill, and get a head. What other people think about you is irrelevant in the bigger scheme of life.

Chapter 6: Negative Friends and Family

Friends and family have the most natural impact on a person's attitude. A negative comment from someone you care for, can bring you down in no time flat. It is very important that you get out and meet new happy go lucky people, who are driven to make the most out of life. Lessen or terminate your time with those who make you feel unhappy about yourself or the world around you.

Many people find it difficult to remove a loved one from their life, even if they know they are a bad influence. Start by seeing them less, and focus on having an exceptional attitude when they are present. When the negative friend or family member is around you in your state of bliss, they will not find this comfortable. They will naturally begin avoiding you. This will do wonders in your life and you should start feeling better immediately.

Quick Tip:

Increase your time with friends and family who are supportive and accepting of who you truly are inside. It is important to surround yourself with those who provide encouragement and unconditional love. If you want to excel in life and create positive thoughts effortlessly, then fill your environment with these types of people. If there is no one in your life that fits this description, then begin by moving forward with a positive attitude and great people will find you.

Chapter 7: Toxic Spouse/Boyfriend/Girlfriend

Having a toxic relationship can be very destructive. They can lead you away from success or put you down in ways that you never thought possible. The person you are inside becomes suppressed, and all goals you once had will go to the waste side.

The emotional rollercoaster is not conducive to a positive mind. As long as the toxic relationship is present, then your life will be one negative experience after another. Rid yourself of this person even if it pains you, and watch as your happiness and self-confidence quickly improves.

Quick Tip:
Relationships should be filled with support and love. Your partner should love you for who you are inside and who you are striving to be in the future. This should be a wonderful time in your life as the two of you are a team. Find a new companion by getting out of the home and doing things that you enjoy. Meeting a person when you are in a place of happiness will increase your chances of finding Mister or Misses right.

10 WAYS TO INCREASE YOUR CHANCES OF FINDING THAT SPECIAL SOMEONE

1. Get out and do activities that you enjoy.

2. Ask people you like to help you find a companion.

3. Be upfront with those who you do meet. Do not hide your true self or you will be wasting your time.

4. Take a class.

5. Volunteer for programs that you believe in.

6. Get involved in your community.

7. Try new experiences that are out of your comfort zone.

8. Join a club.

9. Start a hobby that you can showcase at local/national events and socialize with people with similar interest.

10. If you cannot find an activity that interest you, join a friend in one of theirs.

Chapter 8: Bad Vibes at Work

Working environments tend to leave people feeling depressed, out of place, angry and many times bullied by coworkers. Some companies have an atmosphere so debilitating that anyone who desires a peaceful workplace is forced to leave. It is very common to also experience gossip, poor leadership, sexual harassment, blackmail and shaming.

Quick Tip:

There is no way to change other people's negative attitude, but you can change your own. Make sure that you are not a part of the problem, by ending all involvement in behavior that makes you feel bad or could hurt others. You will soon see that the bullies and poor attitudes steer clear from you, because you are no longer feeding their self-loathing habits.

10 Ways To A Better Work Environment

1. Start by being friendly to everyone regardless of the past.

2. Keep reminding yourself of all the things you appreciate about your life.

3. Stay focused on being productive and completing each task with 100%.

4. Refrain from socializing for more than a few minutes at a time. This will allow you to stay positive and end before anything negative is discussed.

5. Organize your time around work and not socializing with negative co-workers.

6. Create goals that allow you to move forward in life and work.

7. Let negative words bounce-off of you. Simply ignore them and focus on a new and improved life.

8. If someone forces a negative conversation on to you, help them find positive things in their environment to be happy about. They will stop inviting you to their pity party.

9. Don't spread bad vibes yourself. If you are experiencing a setback or challenge, shrug it off and continue to fill your thoughts with the things you appreciate.

10. Stay neutral in group situations. This can be hard if you are surrounded by many toxic attitudes. No matter the intensity of this challenge, you can keep yourself in a positive mind set by giving it your absolute best. Focus on the task and the rest will slide off your back.

❖ However, if this doesn't do the trick finding a new workplace may be crucial for your happiness.

Chapter 9: School House Drama

We've all experienced the side effects of a negative person at school. Perhaps you are being bullied or harassed by someone. Or, a good friend speaks unfavorably about others in your circle and creates drama.

These types of negative people are destructive and drama follows them everywhere. If you're not careful, they can pull you into their chaos, disrupting your focus and sidelining your goals.

5 POWERFUL STRATEGIES TO DEAL WITH NEGATIVE PEOPLE AT SCHOOL

1. **Set boundaries.** Don't feel pressured to sit and listen to a negative person. If you must be around a negative person, try to keep your interactions to a minimum. You can't control the negative behavior, but you can control whether you engage in it.

2. **Avoid complainers.** People who complain about everything will never help you experience happiness. They don't offer solutions, only point out problems. They will knock your ideas and suck you into their emotional pity party. If a friend or classmate display signs of a complainer, change the subject to something positive.

3. **Choose your battles.** Don't be ready to fight every time someone irritates you. Not only will you be seen as argumentative, you'll be welcoming the toxicity into your own life. Rather than going to battle, try ignoring negative comments. Control your emotions and walk away from unnecessary conflict. You'll be respected for taking the high road.

4. **Don't over analyze the situation.** Negative people can behave irrationally. You will waste valuable time and energy if you try to make sense of their actions. Do whatever you can to prevent yourself from becoming emotionally invested in their pointless issues.

5. **Embody positivity.** Your happiness and wellbeing are too important to let anyone's negative opinion or rude comments bring you down. Stay positive and with some time, your positivity will be repugnant to toxic people and they will gradually fall away on their own.

Chapter 10: Rendering Negative People Powerless

It's been said that one bad apple can spoil the whole bunch. It's easy to identify the downer who spreads their poor attitude to everyone else. Their negative thoughts, catastrophic thinking, and fatalistic outlooks can like a disease.

Negative people can also cause problems for us on an individual level. Perhaps it's that vendor who causes you to grit your teeth. Or maybe it's a colleague whom you avoid at all costs. It's important to recognize when these negative individuals intrude in your life in an unwelcoming manner.

Sometimes, we unknowingly give toxic individuals influence over our thoughts, behaviors, and feelings. Whether you spend two hours complaining about that boss you don't like, or you let an angry customer ruin your day, it's important to regain your personal power and straighten your attitude back out.

TOP 4 WAYS TO RENDER NEGATIVE PEOPLE POWERLESS

1. **Time Suckers.** Negative people can monopolize your time - even when they are not with you. It's

easy to waste days dreading about a one hour meeting with a negative person. Combine that with additional hours of venting to a friend after the meeting, and you've just given that person way too much of your time.

Solution. Rather than complaining about people you don't enjoy, choose to strike up conversations about pleasurable topics. Similarly, instead of spending your commute thinking about how much you dislike that person you have to work with, turn on the radio and listen to music that reduces your stress. Take back your power by limiting the amount of time you spend talking about, thinking about, and worrying about unpleasant people.

• Negative people should get the <u>least</u> of our time and energy, yet we often give them the most.

2. **Choose Your Attitude.** Spending time with negative people can be the fastest way to ruin a good mood. Their nasty outlook and gloomy attitude can decrease our motivation and change the way we feel immediately. Allowing a negative person to dictate your emotions gives them too much power.

Solution. Make a conscious effort to fiercely guard your positive attitude from negative intruders. You do not have to live in a state of unhappiness because they choose to. It is your life and you need to take ownership.

3. **Refocus Your Thoughts.** Negative people often have a great influence concerning what we think about even when they are not present. You could be so distracted by your colleague's know-it-all attitude that you can't contribute productively to the meeting. Or you could be kept up all night worried if your classmates will hate your new hairstyle even though you love it.

    Solution. The more time you spend dreading, fretting, worrying, and rehashing, the less time you'll have to devote to more productive thoughts. Make a conscious effort to reduce the amount of mental energy you expend on negative people, or what they may think of you.

4. **Choose to Behave Productively.** Negative people can, if allowed, bring out the worst in us. A normally calm, mild-mannered person may resort to yelling or acting out in unusual ways.

    Solution. Although it can be tempting to blame others for your conduct, this only gives them more power. When you act in a manner that isn't consistent with your usual behavior, accept responsibility for it. Commit to controlling your emotions and staying true to your values, despite your circumstances. View the negative person like a child who is being bad, then you can learn to deal with their outlandish behavior properly.

Chapter 11: Empowering Yourself Through Positive Words

The words you use to express yourself are emotional triggers. The power of words significantly influences your state-of-mind and the attitude you bring forth into every situation. These words either create positive expectations, or they create limiting and negative expectations. Therefore, it's important to choose wisely.

To overcome a negative attitude, you must transform your language. Begin by changing the words you habitually use when in a negative state-of-mind.

YOU CAN DO THIS TWO WAYS

- You can lower the intensity of the negative words you use.
- You can change negative words into positive words.

Initially you could begin using the first option, where you lower the intensity of the words you are expressing. Then once you begin feeling more comfortable with these words, you can then switch to the second option. When you convert a negative word into a positive, you are creating a new and improved perspective of the situation.

There are a lot of possibilities here. All that's required is that you play around with the words you use. Don't settle on one kind of word. Focus on adding a strong sense of happiness and appreciation to your language.

Chapter 12: You Are Who You Associate With

There is a reason why you might have a poor attitude. And that often comes down to the people you associate with. "You are who you run around with," is a saying that wasn't created by accident. The attitude you consistently project into the world, most likely resembles the attitude of your friends. Thus, if their attitude is poor, then your attitude will also be poor. If they always complain, make excuses, blame and focus on problems, then you probably do the same.

Your five closest friends will often mirror your attitude as much as you mirror their attitude. For this very reason, it's critical that you select the people you choose to hang out with very carefully.

ASK YOURSELF THESE QUESTIONS CONCERNING YOUR FRIENDS

- ✓ How do each of my friends influence me?

- ✓ How have each of my friends changed the way I think?

✓ How of each of my friends changed the way I speak to others and myself?

✓ How have each of my friends influenced my state-of-mind & overall confidence?

✓ How have each of my friends influenced the attitude I project out into the world?

✓ Do I complain about the same things they complain about?

✓ Do I blame others in the same way they blame others?

✓ Do I make similar excuses?

✓ Do I feel happy and healthy when I am with each of them?

✓ Do I feel empowered to strive towards my goals when I am around them?

✓ Do I feel like they know the real me, or only someone I am trying to be so I fit in?

If you are being honest with yourself, I think you will find that your friends have a greater influence on your entire life then you initially thought. Choose people who will inspire and challenge you to view your life and circumstances in a positive.

Chapter 13: Meditate on Things You Appreciate

Meditating on things that you appreciate will fill your body and mind with happiness beyond imagine. You can focus on a picture of someone that you admire, or just allow yourself to think of all the wonderful things that you can be thankful for. Finding appreciation for the world around you will dramatically increase your happiness. This exercise doesn't require very much time and is rather simple to do.

Begin by taking 2-30 minutes out of your day, and sit quietly in a room. Close your eyes and think about all the things in your life or future that makes you happy. These are not necessarily monumental ideas, they could simply be the way someone's smile makes you feel. The only requirement is for the idea to make you happy and allow you to focus on how much you appreciate it. Allow the feeling of happiness to consume you for the allotted time, then carry those same feelings with you for the rest of the day.

Really commit yourself to this for at least one month. You can do it anywhere. If you're traveling or something comes up in the morning, you can do meditation in your office, or at the park. Meditation has helped many people to become more peaceful, more focused, less worried, more appreciative and attentive to everything in their life.

2 MINUTE MEDITATION TECHNIQUE IN 10 SIMPLE STEPS

1. **Sit for just two minutes.** If that goes well, increase by another two minutes and do that for a week. If all goes well, mediate for 10 minutes or as long as you need.

2. **Do it first thing each morning.** Even though a morning meditation routine is not required, it does help you start the day off on the right foot.

3. **Don't get caught up in the how.** Most people worry about where to sit, how to sit, what cushion to use. Just start by finding a comfy spot to sit. Later you can worry about finding that perfect place where you will be comfortable for longer.

4. **Check in with how you're feeling.** As you begin your meditation, check to see how you're feeling. How does your body feel? What is the quality of your mind? Busy? Tired? Anxious?

5. **Count your breaths.** Now turn your attention to your breath. Just place the attention on your breath as it comes in, and follow it through your nose all the way down to your lungs. Try counting "one" as you take in the first breath, then "two" as you breathe out. Repeat until you reach "ten" and start over.

6. **Come back when you wander.** A wandering mind is normal. When you notice your mind wandering, simply return to counting your breath.

7. **Develop a loving attitude.** When you are meditating allow yourself to ponder on things that make you happy. This exercise will heighten your

positive outlook instantly. You will feel fulfilled and connected on every level.

8. **Become friends with yourself.** As you get to know yourself, do it with a friendly attitude and do not criticize. This is the exploration of the inner you, the one that needs to be brought out into the open and expressed.

9. **Do a body scan.** Focus your attention on one body part at a time. Start at the soles of your feet, how do those feel? Slowly move to your toes, the tops of your feet, your ankles, all the way to the top of your head.

10. **Notice the light, sounds, energy.** Place your attention the light around you. Just keep your eyes on one spot, and notice the light in the room you're in. Another day, just focus on noticing sounds. Another day, try to focus on the energy in the room.

Chapter 14: Each Day Is a Gift

People tend to take for granted the good that is already present in their lives. For instance, your home, your ability to see or hear, your ability to walk, or anything that currently gives you comfort. In addition, you will need to start finding joy in the small things instead of holding out for big achievements.

Living each day as though is a gift alters your perspective towards just about anything you can fathom. There is always someone out there who is experiencing a life without one of these simple things that others are taking for granted. Keep this in mind when you are presented with negative thoughts or the urge to pity yourself.

Chapter 15: Finding Your Silver-Lining

The idea that "every cloud has a silver lining" represents finding the positive in any situation, no matter how challenging it might be. It's more than just believing that good things are to come, it's an understanding that every negative is actually a positive in disguise. This is one of the greatest ways to change your state-of-mind in a profound way.

HOW TO IDENTIFY A SILVER-LINING IN ANY SITUATION

❖ **How can I use this situation to my advantage?**
Everyone, everything and every experience that comes into your life acts as your teacher. Utilize each lesson to achieve future success.

❖ **How could this positively affect me?**
This is a tough question to ask when your experiencing a painful situation. Greeting discomfort with a positive outlook is essential for changing life around quickly. In the long run, something bad always come baring a seed of good.

❖ **How will this make me stronger?**

You will come to know your true strength when it is put to the test. Use this as a great indicator of your perseverance and ability to push through even the toughest challenges.

❖ **How does this relate to my life purpose?**
Everything that happens to you is needed in order for you to progress to the next level. Life is built on a foundation created through lessons you have learned and completed. The completion of lessons is based on the realization of their true meaning.

❖ **What can I learn from this?**
For your lessons not to repeat, you need to learn what they are teaching you and get on with your life. The things learned from the past will always be applied to your future, so be sure to pay attention.

❖ **What idea does this give me?**
Ask this question five times a day and you will always find inspiration.

❖ **What is the hidden opportunity?**
Growth? Connection? Service? Adventure? Instant reeducation? Reassess your situations. Convert them into something more productive.

❖ **Where else can I use this?**

It's all about learning to bring ideas from one field of knowledge into another. From lessons learned, to utilizing it in the form of an opportunity to create something unique.

Chapter 16: Benefits of Forgiveness

While it is important to forgive our loved ones, it is also very important to forgive ourselves. Studies have shown that people who forgive are happier and healthier than those who hold resentments. They tend to be less angry, feel less hurt, and are more optimistic. They become more compassionate and self-confident and have fulfilling lives.

13 REASONS TO FORGIVE OTHERS AND YOURSELF

1. It starts the healing process.

2. A sense of wholeness and peace.

3. Letting go and moving onward.

4. Finding the silver-lining.

5. Compassion for self and others.

6. A path to healthier relationships.

7. A solution for anxiety and depression.

8. Restoring hope and excitement for the future.

9. Improves self-esteem.

10. Restores faith in yourself and others.

11. Learning from the past.

12. Allows you to see how you contributed to the problem.

13. A way to let go of your pain.

Chapter 17: 20 Affirmations That Are Proven to Work

This one is about changing the conversation with yourself, and about eliminating old harmful thoughts for new fresh and empowering ones. Repeat these affirmations continually, as long as it takes until you have replaced the negative, disgusting, and bad thoughts with happy ones.

20 AFFIRMATIONS FOR A HEALTHIER-HAPPIER MIND

1. I deserve to be happy.

2. I am smart and capable of challenging tasks.

3. I am worthy of love.

4. I see the good in people and situations.

5. I love my life.

6. I love my unique self and appreciate the things that make me different.

7. I am caring and generous.

8. I make great choices.

9. I am strong both physically and mentally.

10. I improve myself every day.

11. I am moving towards my goals.

12. I am going to be a winner today.

13. I am creating good habits, eating healthy and exercising.

14. I learn easily.

15. My past lessons have prepared me for the future.

16. I appreciate my life in every way possible.

17. I chose to only see the good in my surroundings.

18. I love experiencing life from my unique perspective.

19. I live life to the fullest every moment of the day.

20. If I can do anything that I set my mind on.

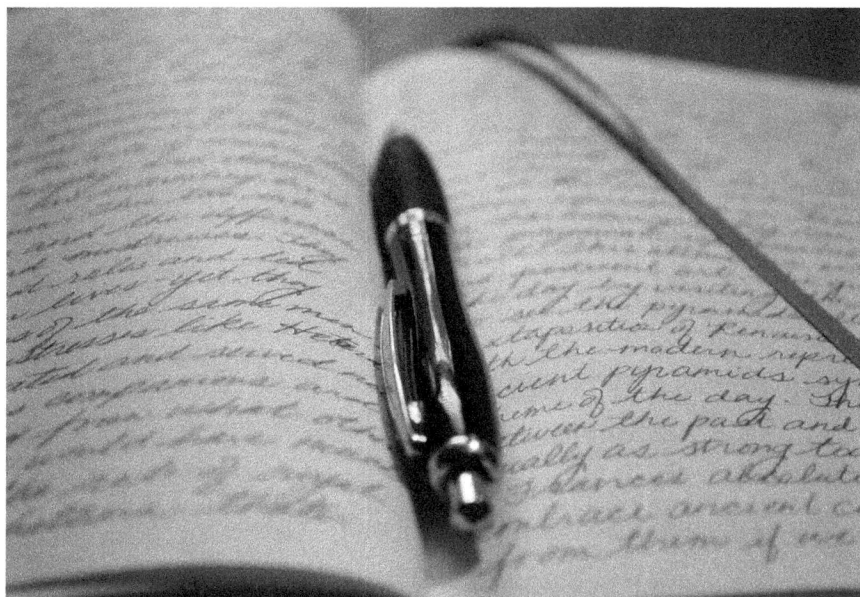

Chapter 18: Appreciation Journal

Creating an Appreciation Journal is fun and easy. This consists of writing down a list of things that you are grateful for and appreciate. You can do this first thing in the morning, or before going to bed at night. Use a notebook or diary to keep track of your writings.

Appreciation works its magic by serving as an antidote to negativity. It's like white blood cells for our mind, protecting us from anger, entitlement, depression, stress, sadness and fear.

8 WAYS YOU BENEFIT FROM THE APPRECIATION JOURNAL

1. Lowers stress.

2. Feel calm at night.

3. Gain a new perspective of what is important to you and what you truly appreciate.

4. Gain clarity on what you want to have more of in your life, and what you need to purge.

5. Helps you focus on what really matters.

6. Helps you learn more about yourself and become self-aware.

7. Your journal is a safe zone for your eyes only, so you can write anything you feel without judgment.

8. On days when you feel blue, read back through your journal to restore a positive attitude.

MAINTAINING YOUR JOURNAL

- Plan to write in your appreciation journal every night for 5-15 minutes before bed, upon waking or anytime during the day. Set an alarm reminder on your phone or schedule it in your calendar.

- Keep your journal by your nightstand so you will see it before going to sleep. Your journal may even become a symbol of gratitude so that when you look over at it, you will feel a sense of appreciation spiking your happiness levels.

- Work on describing what you appreciate in more detail. By focusing more on each topic, you are increasing the amount of happiness that it brings you.

Chapter 19: The 30 Day Challenge

Take the 30-day challenge. This exercise will change your entire life, increase your happiness and health. Go 30-days without complaining, criticizing, gossiping or giving into negative thoughts.

❖ **The rules are simple: Only think positive thoughts and nothing else.**

MAGIC IN 30-DAYS

- Eliminates stress.

- Increases energy and enthusiasm.

- Sleep better.

- Enjoy healthier relationships.

- Be a better friend or parent.

- Accomplish more in less time.

- Clearly see the future.

- Feel and appear more attractive.

- Increased self-awareness.

- Ability to inspire others.

- Make better decisions.

- Focus with precision.

- People are drawn to your positive personality.

- Sudden interest in new activities.

- Have more fun with friends and family.

- Increased memory.

- Driven to accomplish goals.

- Become the friend everyone wants.

- Healthier outlook on life.

- Move on from issues that once held you back.

- Better grades and increased work performance.

- Increased creativity.

- And so much more......

Chapter 20: Final Thoughts

Once you become set on being positive, looking for things to appreciate will come with ease. You will find that you begin to enjoy simple pleasures and things that you previously took for granted.

Try to be grateful towards even the most difficult and challenging situations that arise in your life. It is often through these situations that we experience the most profound growth. You can learn to view each obstacle as an opportunity to develop a new quality, strength, skill, insight, or wisdom.

www.ingramcontent.com/pod-product-compliance
Lightning Source LLC
Chambersburg PA
CBHW060051050426
42448CB00011B/2394